This Turtles Coloring Book
Belongs To

Turtles
Kids and Adults Coloring Book

Reptiles Animal Coloring Book for Turtle Lovers

This incredible Kids and Adult Coloring Book for turtle lover's.
It has over **60** hand-painted pictures of turtles to make your mind feel pleasures.

Coloring all these pictures will help someone to get rid of stress and this coloring book will be useful to enjoy the time.

Reptiles Animal coloring books for adults,
adult coloring books sea turtles,
coloring books for grown-ups,
reptiles animal designs coloring book,
sea turtle coloring book.

A must have for people that love Turtles - Now get your Reptiles animal adult coloring book!

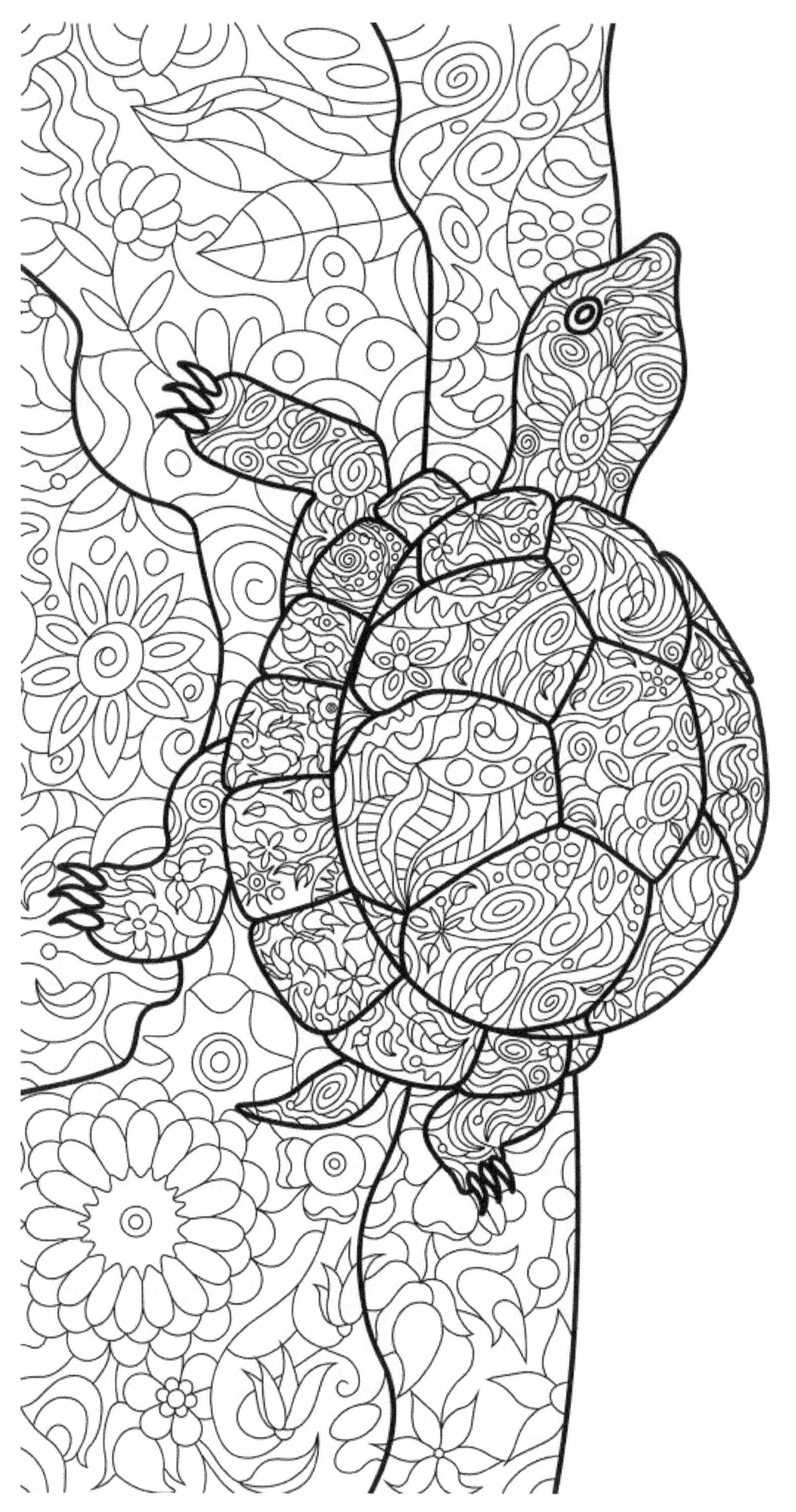

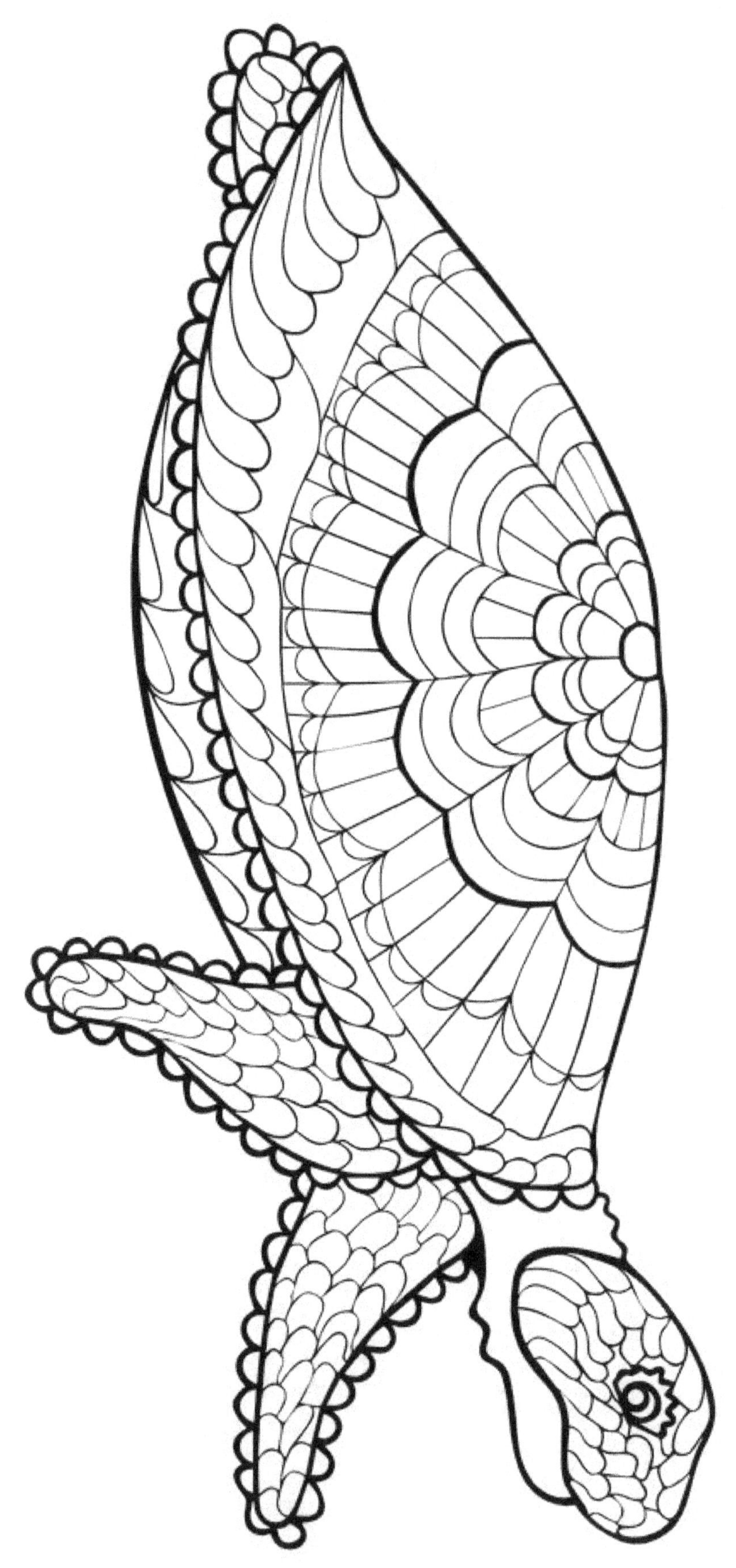

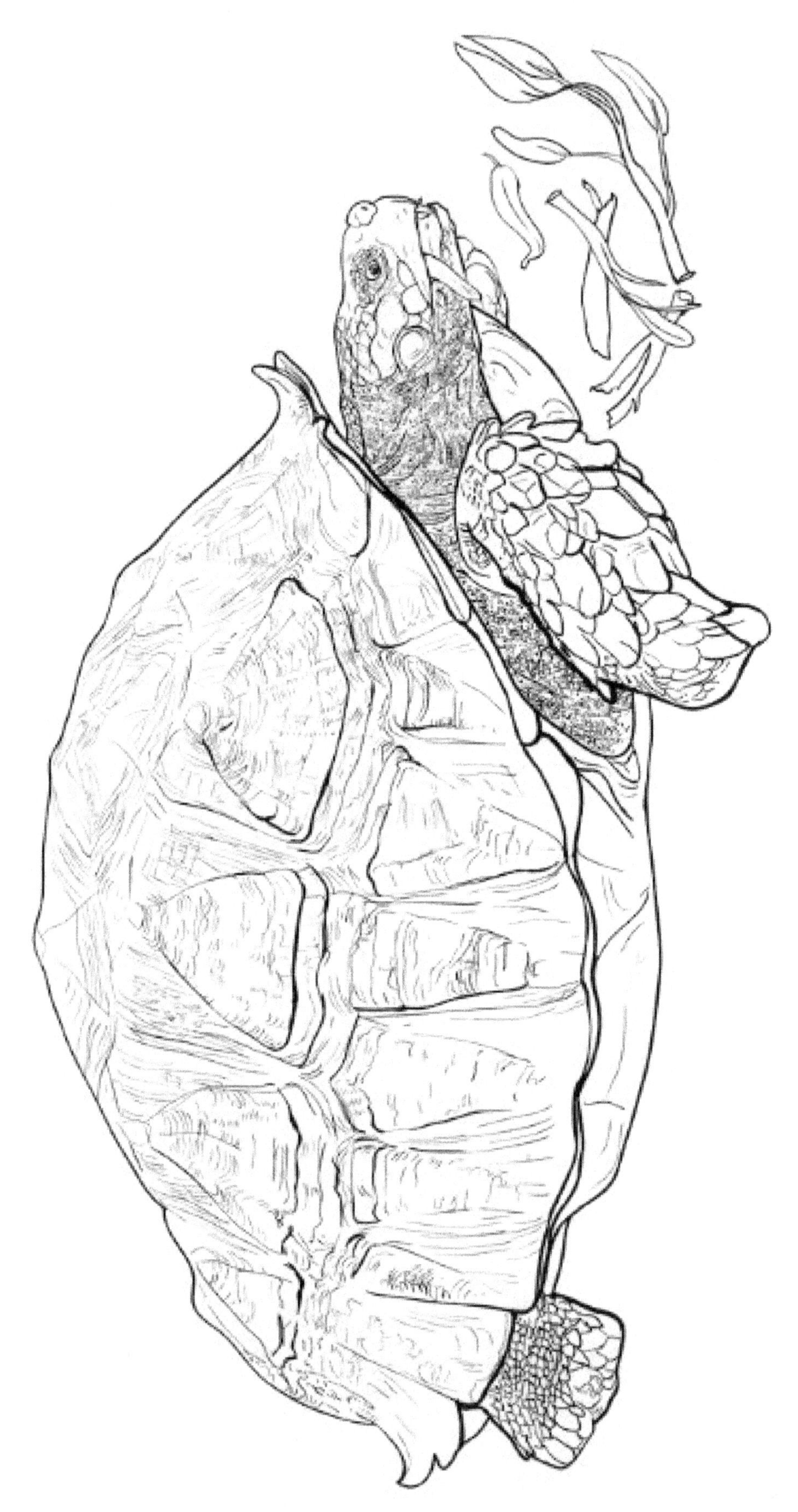

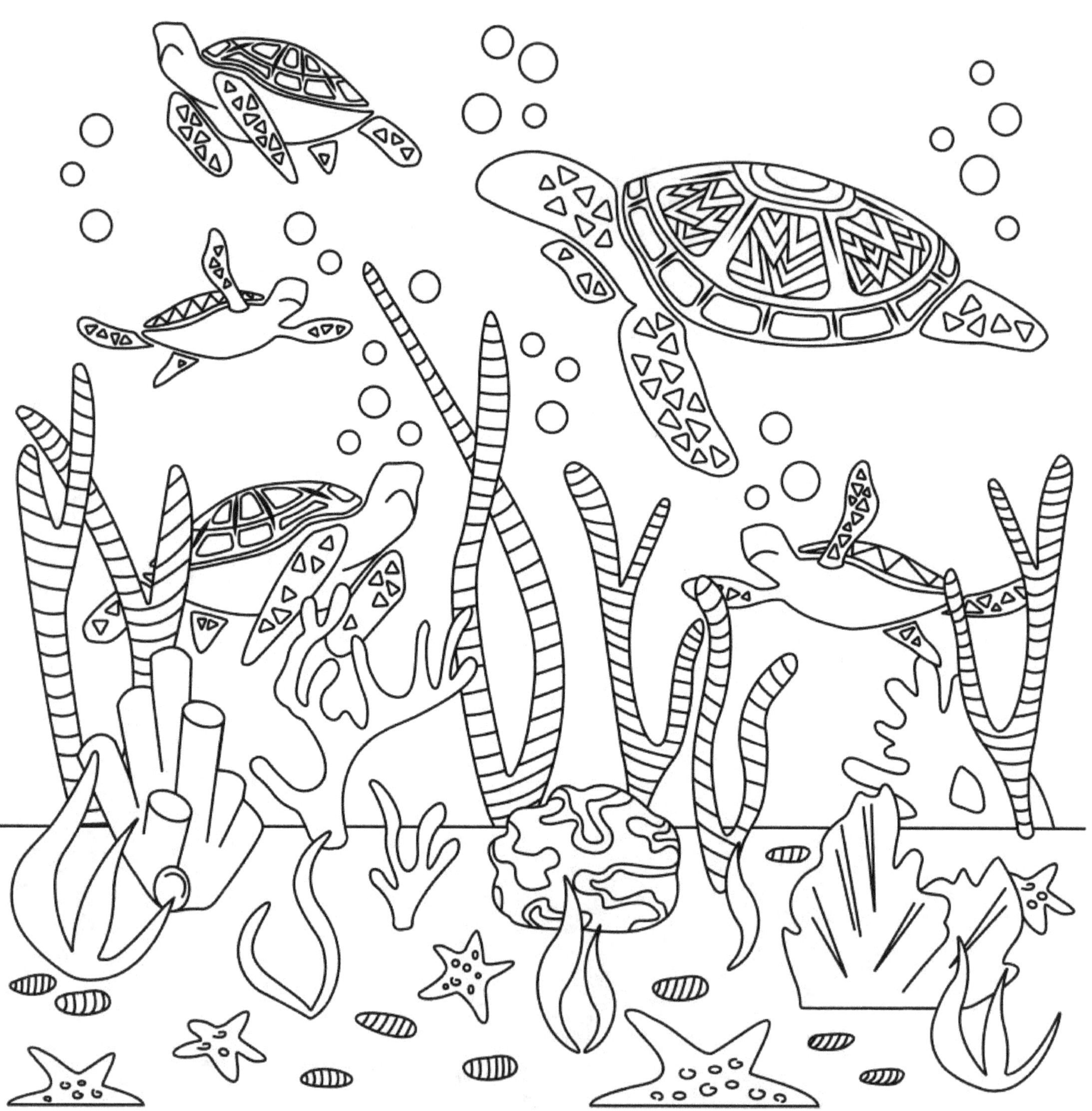

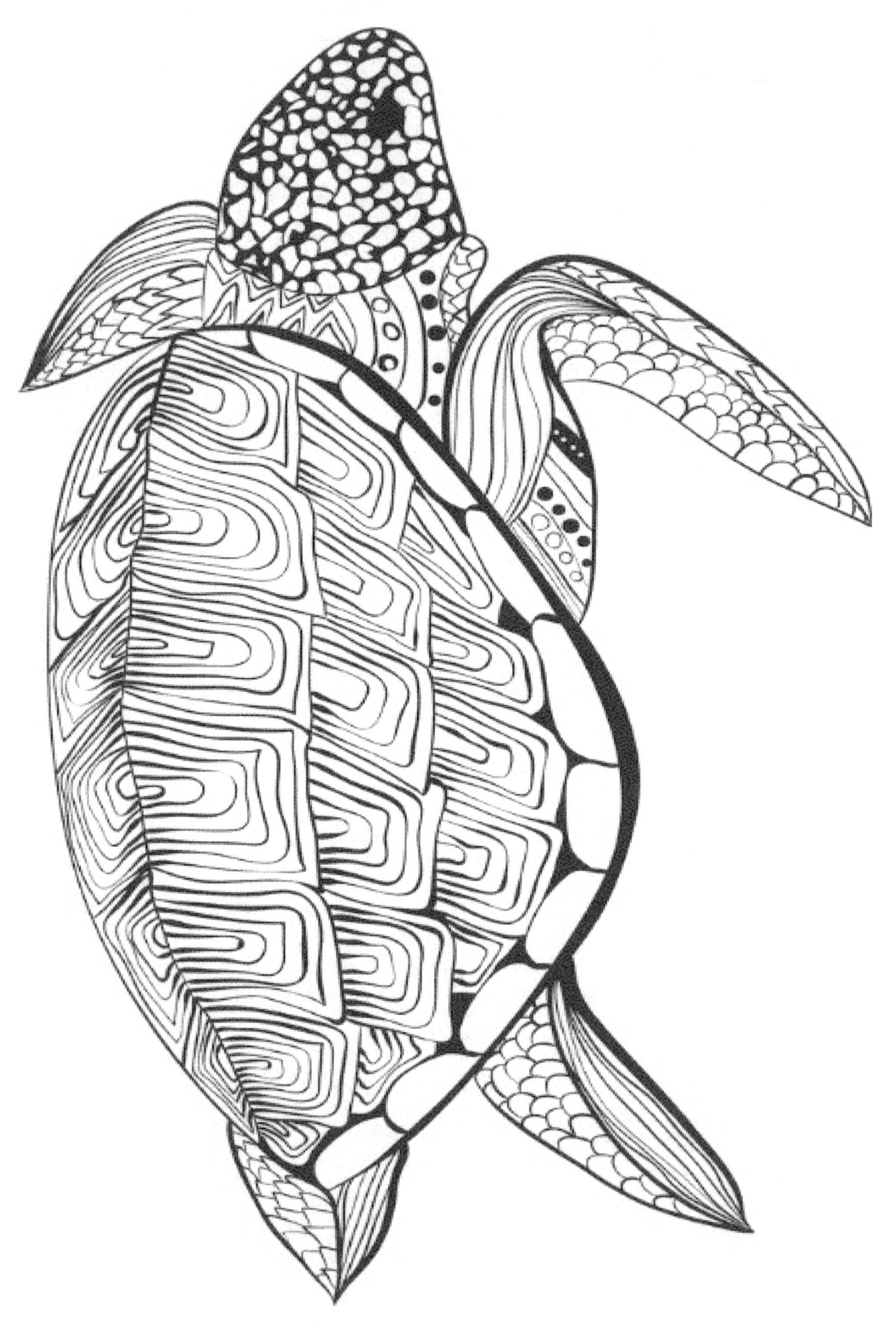

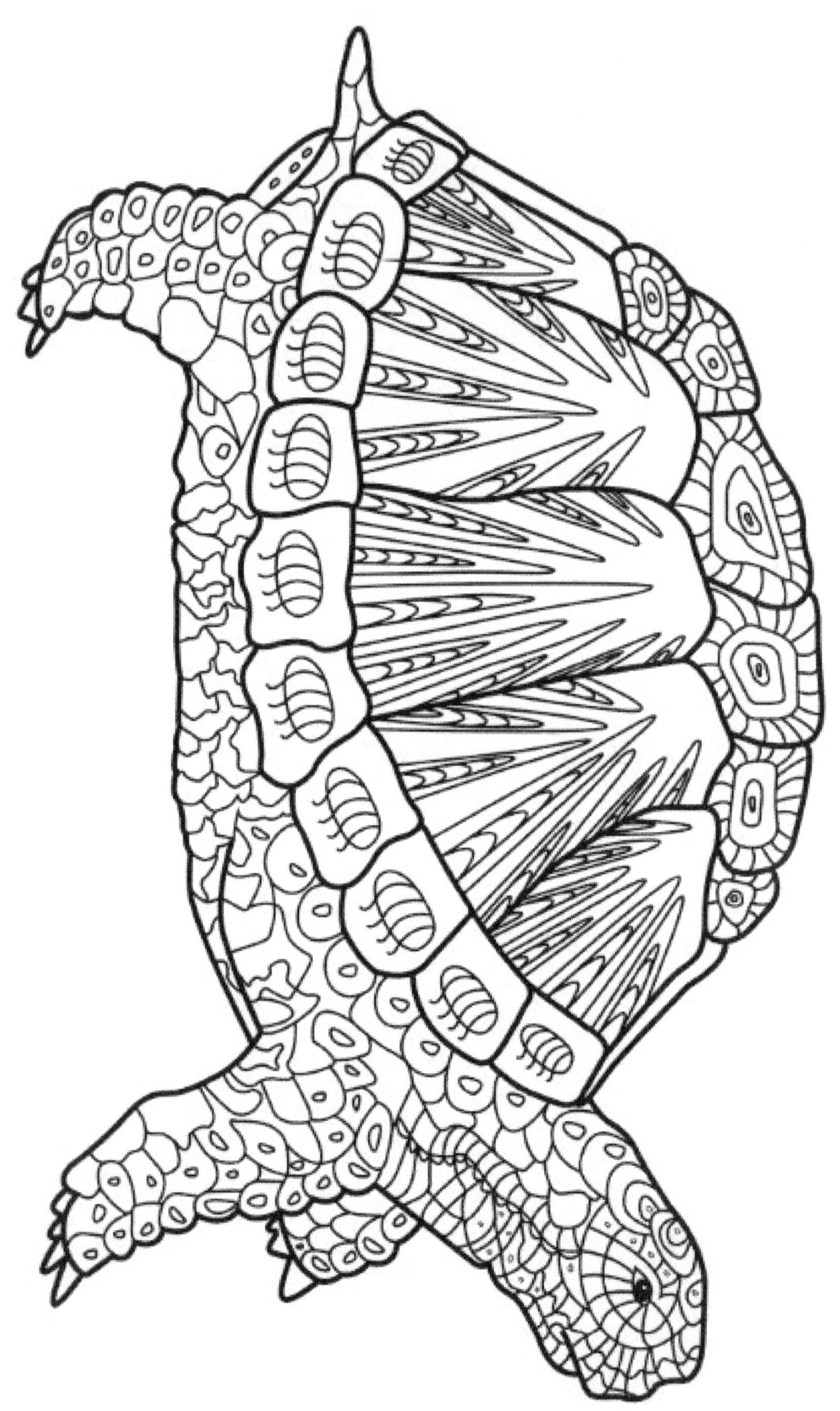

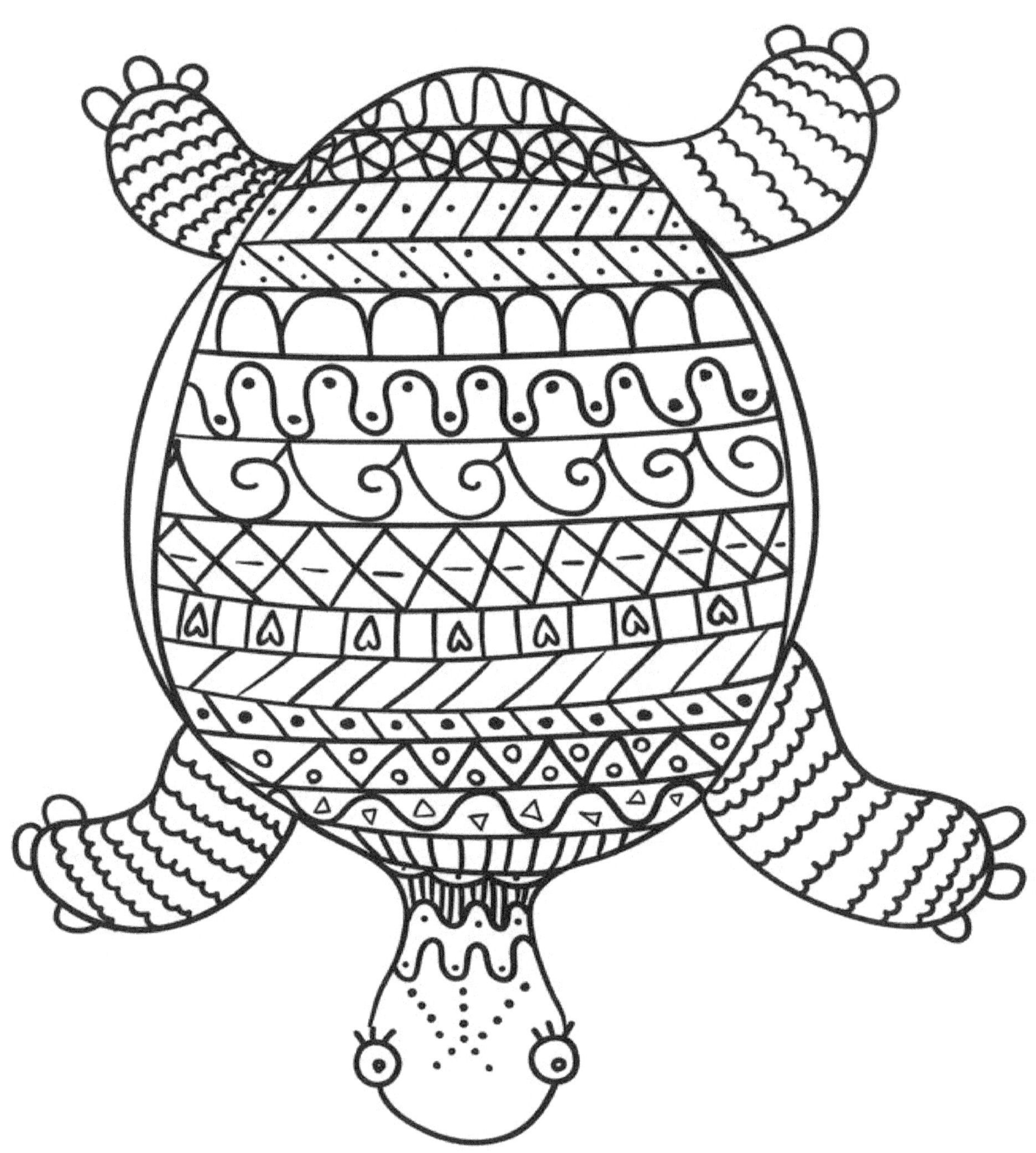

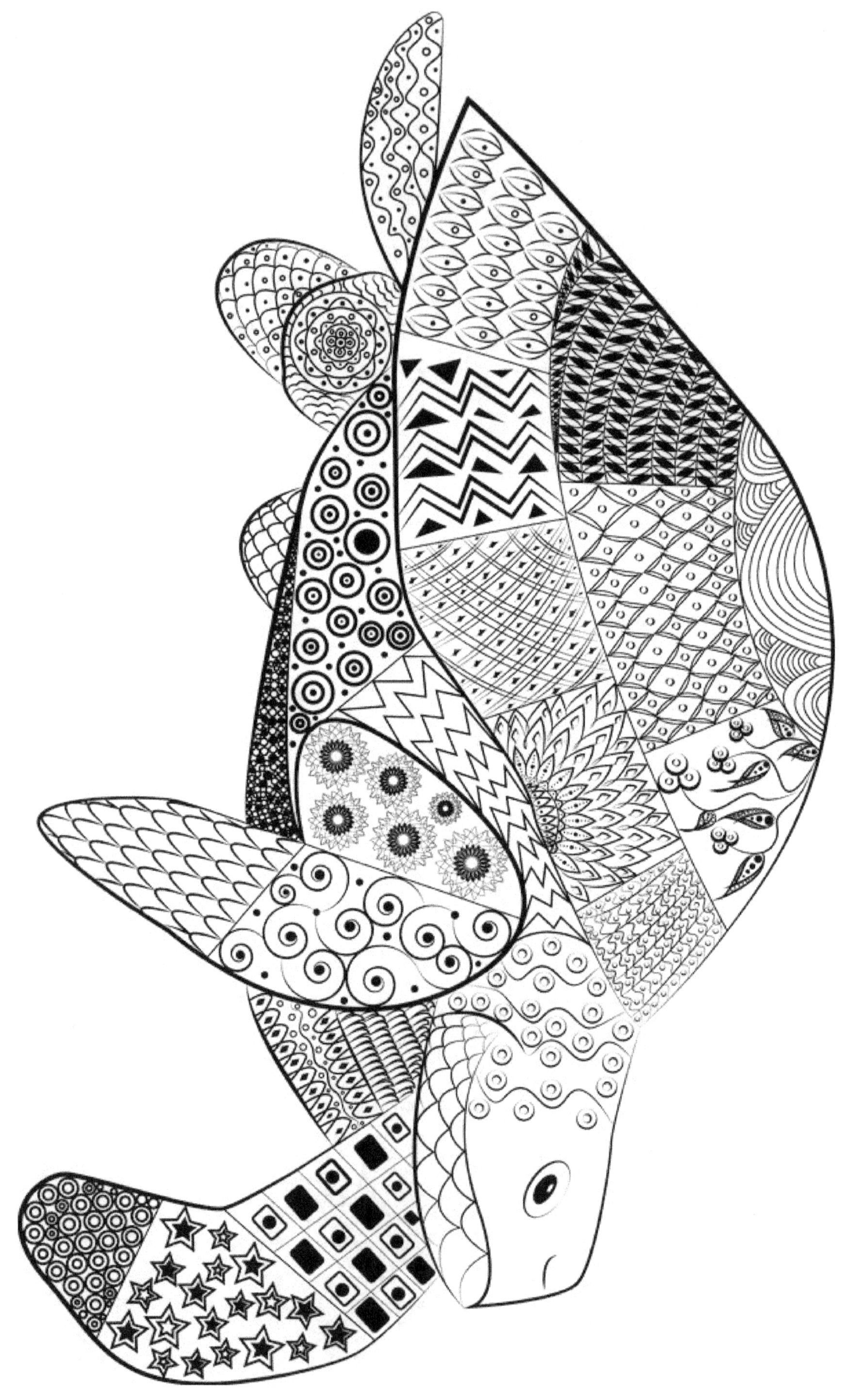

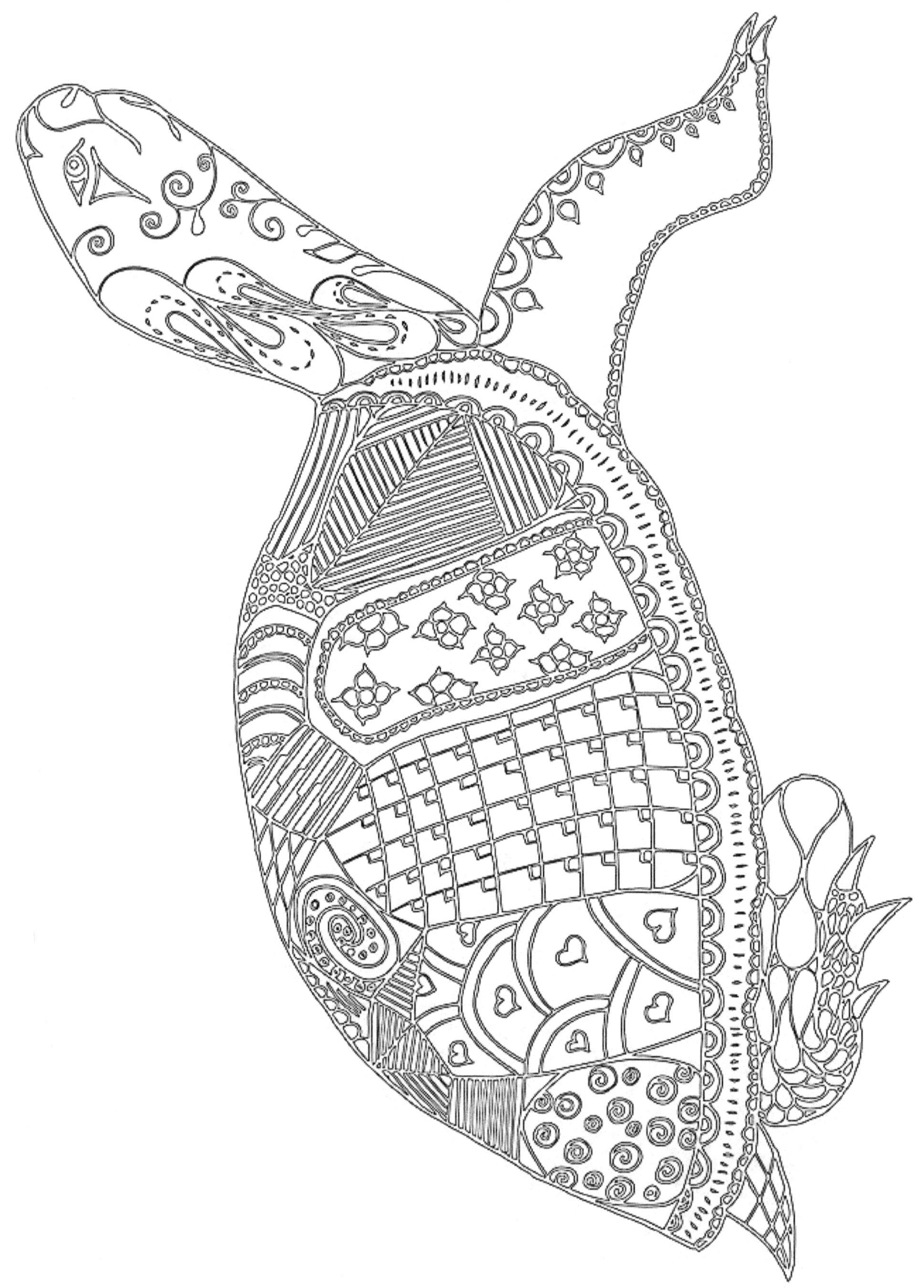

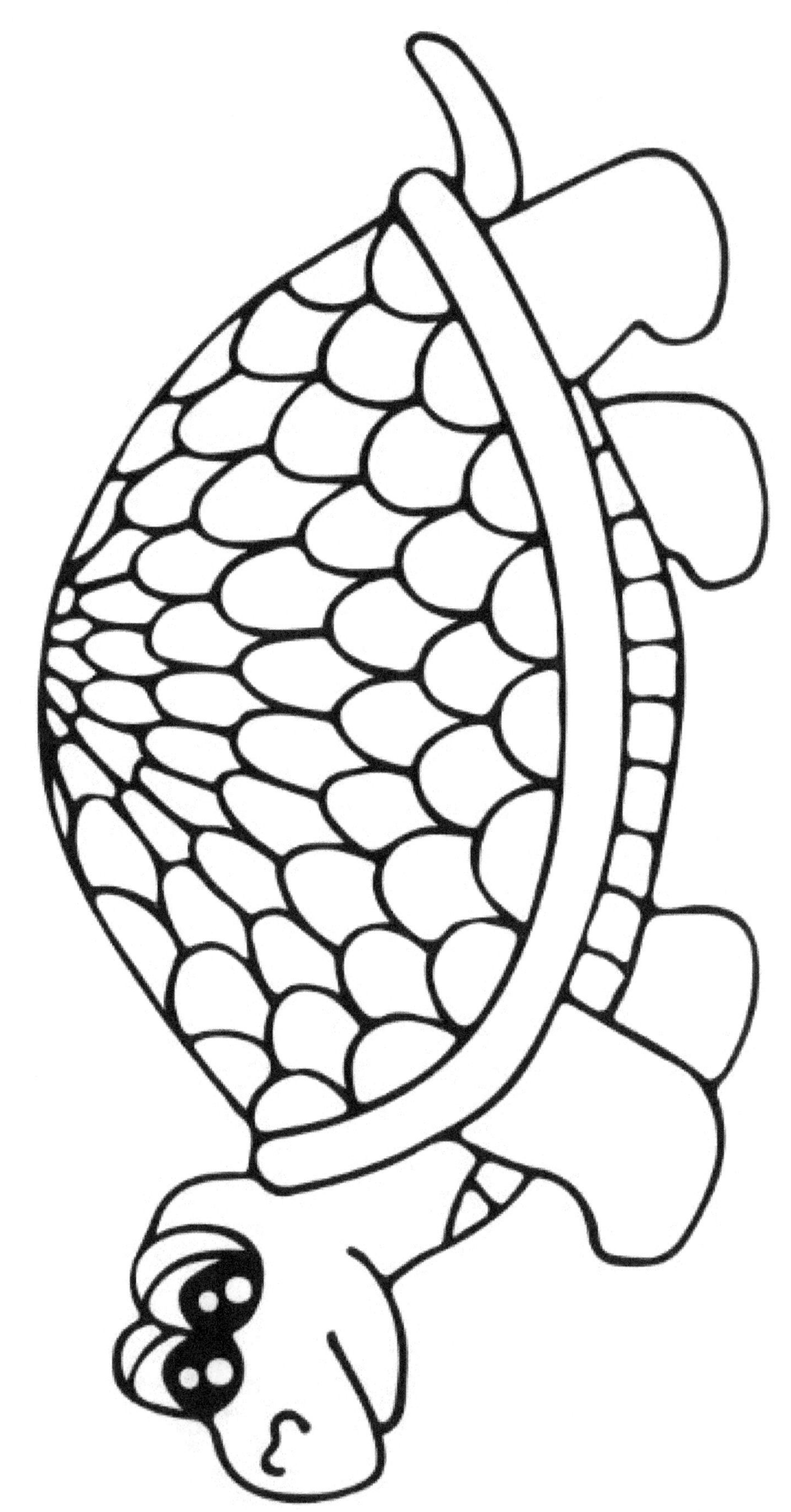

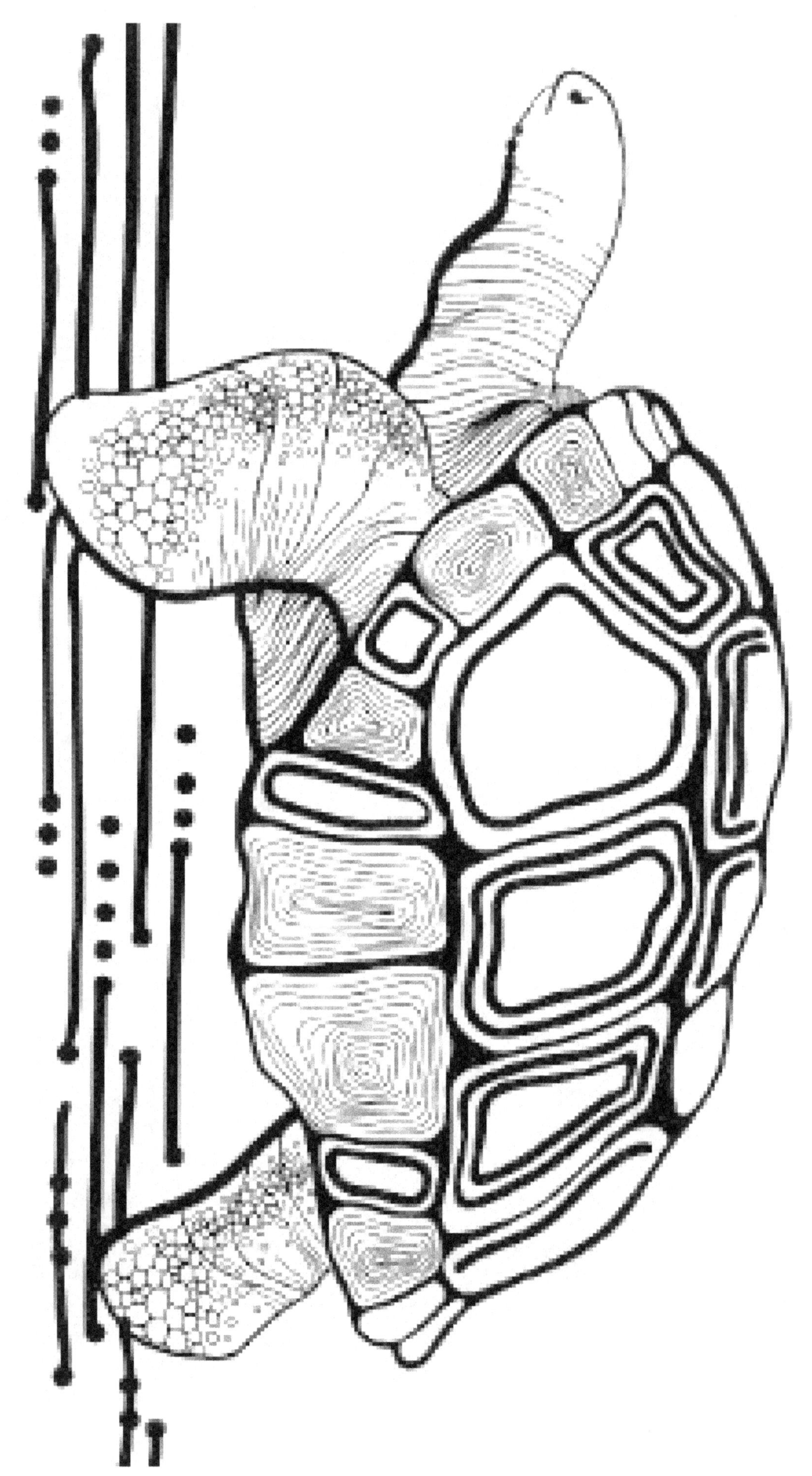

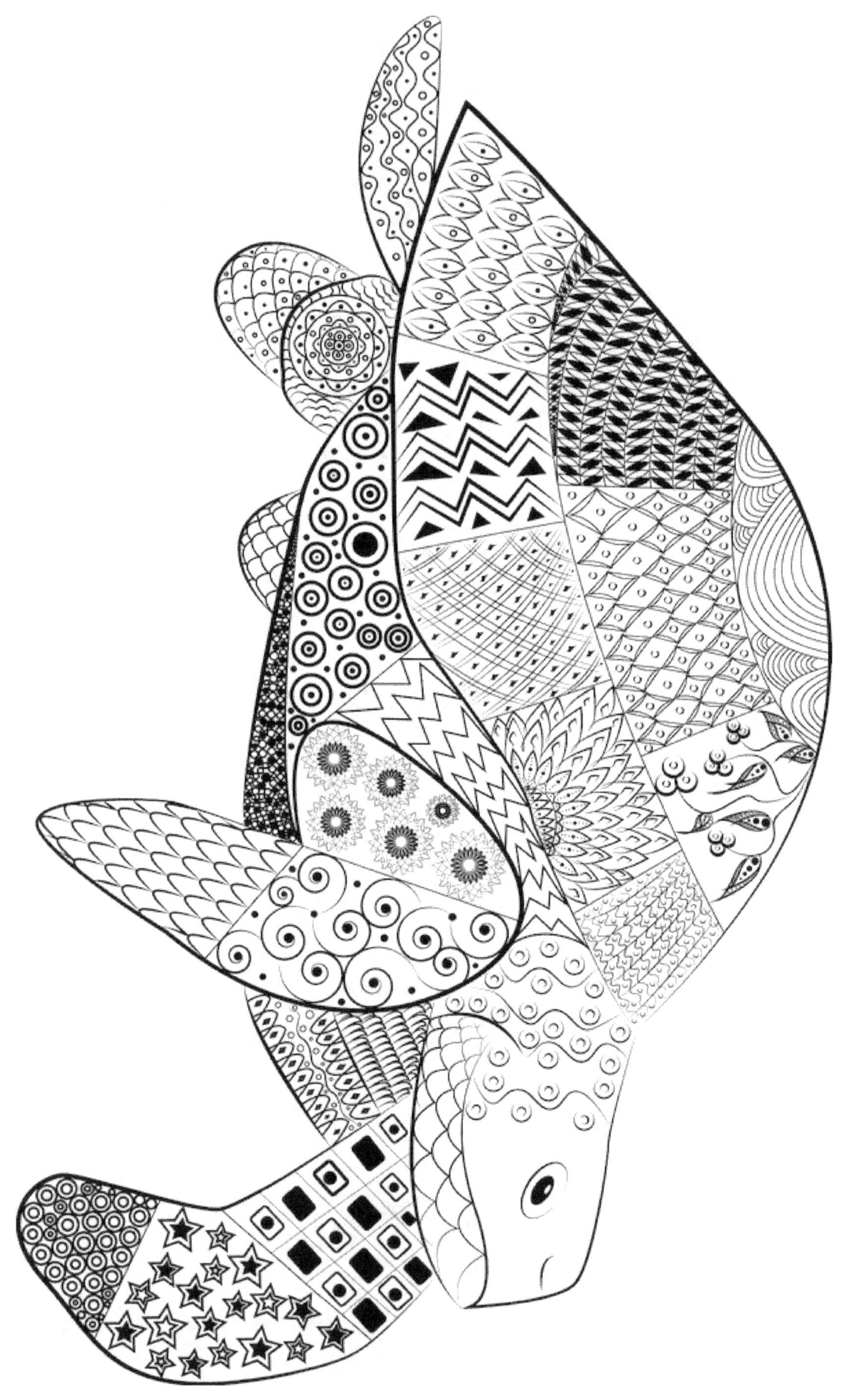

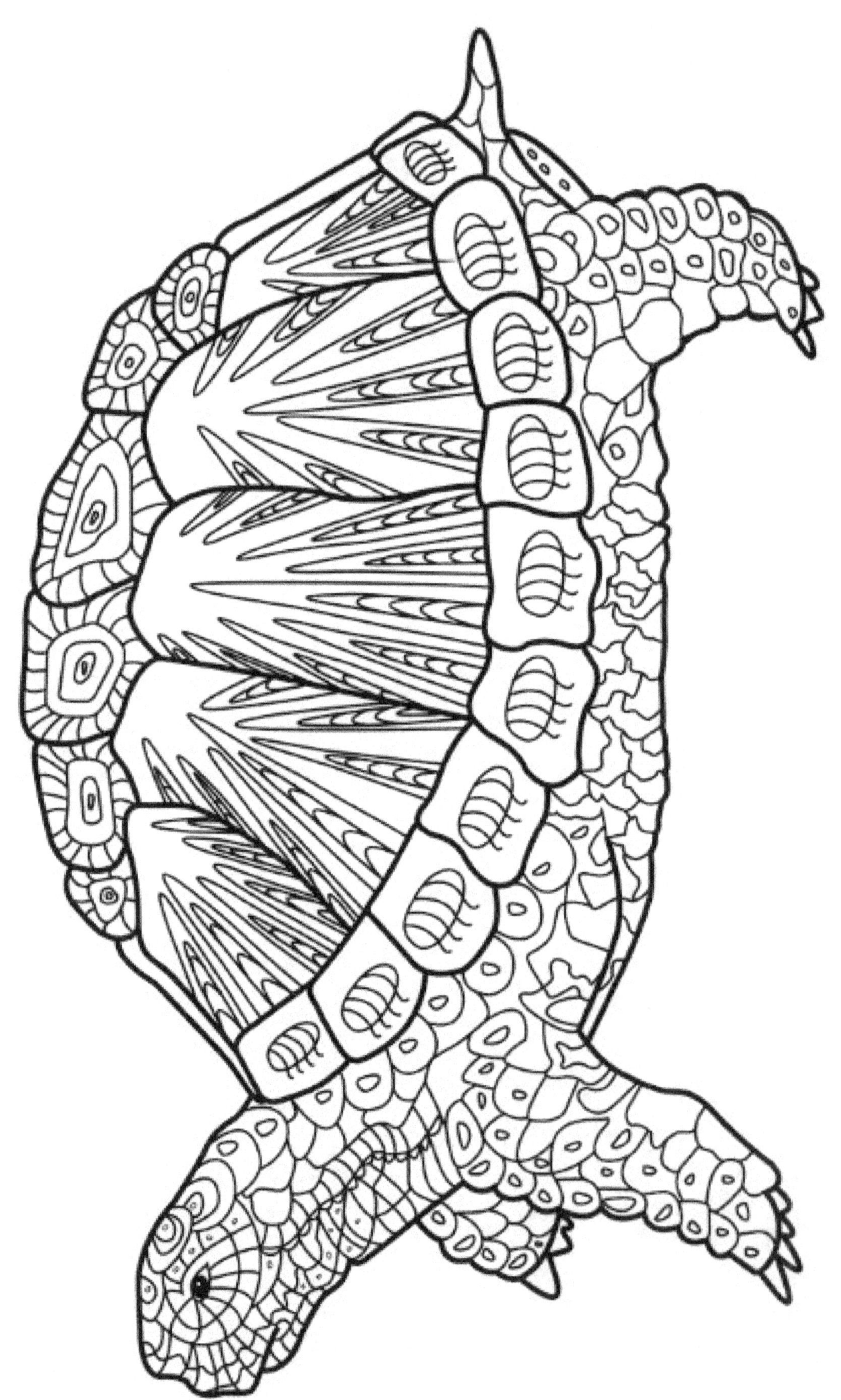

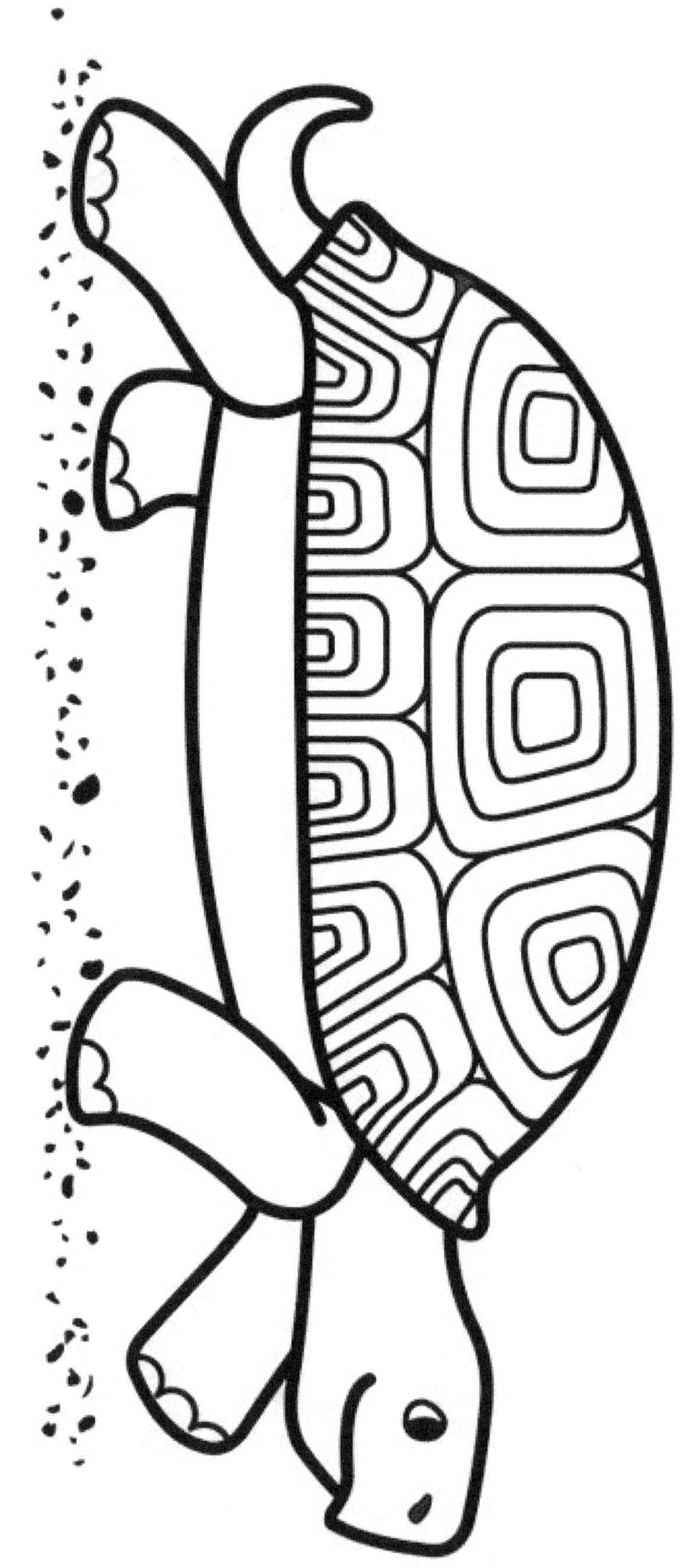

9 798702 285740